FRANCIS FRITH'S

VILLAGES OF SURREY

PHOTOGRAPHIC MEMORIES

DAVID ROSE is a newspaper journalist and local history writer
who has always lived in Guildford. He was educated at his local
comprehensive school, and his love of the Surrey countryside
and its history has meant that since his teens in the 1970s he has
enjoyed exploring all parts of the county.

FRANCIS FRITH'S
PHOTOGRAPHIC MEMORIES

VILLAGES OF SURREY

PHOTOGRAPHIC MEMORIES

DAVID ROSE

First published in the United Kingdom in 2004 by
Frith Book Company Ltd

Paperback Edition 2004
ISBN 1-85937-914-1

British Library Cataloguing in Publication Data

Francis Frith's Villages of Surrey - Photographic Memories
David Rose
ISBN 1-85937-914-1

Frith Book Company Ltd
Frith's Barn, Teffont,
Salisbury, Wiltshire SP3 5QP
Tel: +44 (0) 1722 716 376
Email: info@francisfrith.co.uk
www.francisfrith.co.uk

Printed and bound in Great Britain

Front Cover: **GODSTONE**, *Church Lane 1905* 53284t
Frontispiece: **WONERSH**, *Wonersh Common* 41776

*The colour-tinting is for illustrative purposes only, and is not intended
to be historically accurate*

AS WITH ANY HISTORICAL DATABASE THE FRITH ARCHIVE IS
CONSTANTLY BEING CORRECTED AND IMPROVED AND THE
PUBLISHERS WOULD WELCOME INFORMATION ON OMISSIONS OR
INACCURACIES

CONTENTS

FRANCIS FRITH
VICTORIAN PIONEER

FRANCIS FRITH, founder of the world-famous photographic archive, was a complex and multi-talented man. A devout Quaker and a highly successful Victorian businessman, he was philosophical by nature and pioneering in outlook.

By 1855 he had already established a wholesale grocery business in Liverpool, and sold it for the astonishing sum of £200,000, which is the equivalent today of over £15,000,000. Now a very rich man, he was able to indulge his passion for travel. As a child he had pored over travel books written by early explorers, and his fancy and imagination had been stirred by family holidays to the sublime mountain regions of Wales and Scotland. 'What lands of spirit-stirring and enriching scenes and places!' he had written. He was to return to these scenes of grandeur in later years to 'recapture the thousands of vivid and tender memories', but with a different purpose. Now in his thirties, and captivated by the new science of photography, Frith set out on a series of pioneering journeys up the Nile and to the Near East that occupied him from 1856 until 1860.

INTRIGUE AND EXPLORATION

These far-flung journeys were packed with intrigue and adventure. In his life story, written when he was sixty-three, Frith tells of being held captive by bandits, and of fighting 'an awful midnight battle to the very point of surrender with a deadly pack of hungry, wild dogs'. Wearing flowing Arab costume, Frith arrived at Akaba by camel sixty years before Lawrence of Arabia, where he encountered 'desert princes and rival sheikhs, blazing with jewel-hilted swords'.

He was the first photographer to venture beyond the sixth cataract of the Nile. Africa was still the mysterious 'Dark Continent', and Stanley and Livingstone's historic meeting was a decade into the future. The conditions for picture taking confound belief. He laboured for hours in his wicker dark-room in the sweltering heat of the desert, while the volatile chemicals fizzed dangerously in their trays. Back in London he exhibited his photographs and was 'rapturously cheered' by members of the Royal Society. His reputation as a photographer was made overnight.

VENTURE OF A LIFE-TIME

Characteristically, Frith quickly spotted the opportunity to create a new business as a specialist publisher of photographs. He lived in an era of immense and sometimes violent change.

For the poor in the early part of Victoria's reign work was exhausting and the hours long, and people had precious little free time to enjoy themselves. Most had no transport other than a cart or gig at their disposal, and rarely travelled far beyond the boundaries of their own town or village. However, by the 1870s the railways had threaded their way across the country, and Bank Holidays and half-day Saturdays had been made obligatory by Act of Parliament. All of a sudden the working man and his family were able to enjoy days out and see a little more of the world.

With typical business acumen, Francis Frith foresaw that these new tourists would enjoy having souvenirs to commemorate their days out. In 1860 he married Mary Ann Rosling and set out on a new career: his aim was to photograph every city, town and village in Britain. For the next thirty years he travelled the country by train and by pony and trap, producing fine photographs of seaside resorts and beauty spots that were keenly bought by millions of Victorians. These prints were painstakingly pasted into family albums and pored over during the dark nights of winter, rekindling precious memories of summer excursions.

THE RISE OF FRITH & CO

Frith's studio was soon supplying retail shops all over the country. To meet the demand he gathered about him a small team of photographers, and published the work of independent artist-photographers of the calibre of Roger Fenton and Francis Bedford. In order to gain some understanding of the scale of Frith's business one only has to look at the catalogue issued by Frith & Co in 1886: it runs to some 670 pages, listing not only many thousands of views of the British Isles but also many photographs of most European countries, and China, Japan, the USA and Canada - note the sample page shown on page 9 from the hand-written Frith & Co ledgers recording the pictures. By 1890 Frith had created the greatest specialist photographic publishing company in the world, with over 2,000 sales outlets - more than the combined number that Boots and WH Smith have today! The picture on the next page shows the Frith & Co display board at Ingleton in the Yorkshire Dales (left of window). Beautifully constructed with a mahogany frame and gilt inserts, it could display up to a dozen local scenes.

POSTCARD BONANZA

The ever-popular holiday postcard we know today took many years to develop. In 1870 the Post Office issued the first plain cards, with a pre-printed stamp on one face. In 1894 they allowed other publishers' cards to be sent through the mail with an attached adhesive halfpenny stamp. Demand grew rapidly, and in 1895 a new size of postcard was permitted called the court card, but there was little room for illustration. In 1899, a year after Frith's death, a new card measuring 5.5 x 3.5 inches became the standard format, but it was not until 1902 that the divided back came into being, so that the address and message could be on one face and a full-size illustration on the other. Frith & Co were in the vanguard of postcard development: Frith's sons Eustace and Cyril continued their father's monumental task, expanding the number of views offered to the public and recording more and more places in Britain, as the

8

coasts and countryside were opened up to mass travel.

Francis Frith had died in 1898 at his villa in Cannes, his great project still growing. The archive he created continued in business for another seventy years. By 1970 it contained over a third of a million pictures showing 7,000 British towns and villages.

FRANCIS FRITH'S LEGACY

Frith's legacy to us today is of immense significance and value, for the magnificent archive of evocative photographs he created provides a unique record of change in the cities, towns and villages throughout Britain over a century and more. Frith and his fellow studio photographers revisited locations many times down the years to update their views, compiling for us an enthralling and colourful pageant of British life and character.

We are fortunate that Frith was dedicated to recording the minutiae of everyday life. For it is this sheer wealth of visual data, the painstaking chronicle of changes in dress, transport, street layouts, buildings, housing, engineering and landscape that captivates us so much today. His remarkable images offer us a powerful link with the past and with the lives of our ancestors.

THE VALUE OF THE ARCHIVE TODAY

Computers have now made it possible for Frith's many thousands of images to be accessed almost instantly. Frith's images are increasingly used as visual resources, by social historians, by researchers into genealogy and ancestry, by architects and town planners, and by teachers involved in local history projects.

In addition, the archive offers every one of us an opportunity to examine the places where we and our families have lived and worked down the years. Highly successful in Frith's own era, the archive is now, a century and more on, entering a new phase of popularity. Historians consider the Francis Frith Collection to be of prime national importance. It is the only archive of its kind remaining in private ownership. Francis Frith's archive is now housed in an historic timber barn in the beautiful village of Teffont in Wiltshire. Its founder would not recognize the archive office as it is today. In place of the many thousands of dusty boxes containing glass plate negatives and an all-pervading odour of photographic chemicals, there are now ranks of computer screens. He would be amazed to watch his images travelling round the world at unimaginable speeds through internet lines.

The archive's future is both bright and exciting. Francis Frith, with his unshakeable belief in making photographs available to the greatest number of people, would undoubtedly approve of what is being done today with his lifetime's work. His photographs depicting our shared past are now bringing pleasure and enlightenment to millions around the world a century and more after his death.

VILLAGES OF SURREY
AN INTRODUCTION

RICH IN CONTRASTS and steeped in history, Surrey is home to more than a million people, yet it is still not overcrowded. Less than 40 miles across from east to west and 25 miles from north to south, it covers some 650 square miles, and is therefore one of the UK's smaller counties. Split into 11 local authorities, it has a number of towns, yet no cities. On the other hand, there are plenty of communities living in villages of all shapes and sizes surrounded by a rich rural landscape.

The inhabitants of its villages do not now depend on agriculture and cottage industries for their subsistence, although farming is still important in a number of areas. Many of today's villagers may well travel further afield to work,

LEIGH, *The School 1904* 52197

but they still regard the place they return to from their daily commute as their home and as a place to raise children. It is more often than not the village in which they spend their leisure time, taking an active part in local life - but mostly at weekends, it has to be admitted.

The county is certainly struggling to find suitable sites for the thousands of extra homes demanded by the Government, but the green belt policy still ensures that its beauty spots, areas of special scientific interest and other sensitive places are not developed. For this reason Surrey has a wealth of natural as well as spectacular open spaces available to everyone, much of which is owned by the National Trust or the local authorities.

Today's inhabitants of Surrey's villages are a lot different from those of a couple of generations ago. We are, of course, as a society more mobile; we own our own homes, and we have greater spending powers. This book, therefore, is an excellent opportunity to view and reflect on the changes that have taken place since the times when the poorly paid local farm worker or labourer and his family would have hardly travelled more than a dozen miles away from their village during their lifetime. It is also an opportunity to trace the history of Surrey's villages, noting some of the developments and events that have shaped their existence. The earliest photographs in this book were taken towards the end of the 19th century, and continue through to the 1960s. You may be surprised to see a view that has changed dramatically, or perhaps one that has altered very little.

Some villages have grown and are now little more than suburbs of a nearby town; others still command a lone position surrounded by countryside. However, I believe I am right in

WONERSH, *The Village 1932* 84959

saying that they have all retained some sort of independence - whether through an active parish council or a dedicated group of locals keen to preserve and maintain the heart and soul of their respective community. These are communities that can be as fiercely independent as in the days when the local lord of the manor or the squire controlled that village.

Surrey's villages vary greatly. Whether surrounding a green, hugging a through road, or straddling a stream or river, their existence goes back hundreds if not thousands of years. Many buildings survive that are made of local materials, such as the Bargate stone cottages found in the south-western part of the county, or those constructed of red bricks made from locally-dug clay and fired in kilns within a few miles of where they have been used. Half-timbered houses from the medieval period, albeit much altered and added to over the years, survive alongside some of the county's grander buildings. Some of these reflect the style of the late 19th- and early 20th-century Arts and Crafts movement, and were designed by noted architects such as Edwin Landseer Lutyens and Richard Norman Shaw.

We may not know who they were who, long ago, designed and built Surrey's multitude of historic churches, but they have left their mark on the landscape. The Victorian period saw a great deal of church renovation; some of it is regarded by today's experts as appalling and nothing short of vandalism, but some Victorian architects did excellent work. One of these was

EAST MOLESEY, *The Lock 1896* 38347

12

Henry Woodyer, who lived near Bramley, and who has to his name a number of exemplary church renovations. His major work was the design of that well-known public school, Cranleigh School, but he also designed several Surrey village schools, rectories and vicarages. And like Lutyens, his style is fairly easy to spot.

As in so many parts of the UK, the coming of the railways forced change on those Surrey villages that had hardly altered for centuries. Since Surrey was so close to London, the railways soon brought wealthy people into the county's enchanting and then often desolate countryside in search of a place to build a home away from the smoky and polluted capital.

The scientist and mountaineer Professor John Tyndall discovered Hindhead in the early 1880s, marvelling at its clear air so similar to that found in Switzerland. It was not long before other eminent Victorians and also Edwardians made a base in the county. The author of 'Peter Pan', James Matthew Barrie, lived for a while at Tilford; the writer Sir Arthur Conan Doyle was another Hindhead resident; the composer Ralph Vaughan Williams lived near Leith Hill; George Meredith, the poet and novelist, had a home at the foot of Box Hill near Mickleham; and the Welsh-born American journalist, Henry Morton Stanley, who tracked down the explorer David Livingstone in Africa, made his home near Pirbright and is buried in the churchyard there.

Surrey has an amazing number of different natural features and landscapes for a county so small. It is also one of the most, if not the most, wooded county in the country. It is bordered by the great River Thames to the north, and has thirteen per cent of the total heathland found in England. Not far from the heaths are areas of clay that butt up to the chalk ridge of the North Downs, which itself runs across the whole of the county from east to west. Just to the south and parallel to the Downs are the greensand hills that

NUTFIELD, *The Village c1955* N53012

13

include Leith Hill, the highest point in south-east England. Further south towards the Sussex border and the Weald is another area dominated by clay soils. The Rivers Wey and Mole add further changes to the landscape; they run right through the clay, sand and chalk in roughly a south to north direction, eventually flowing into the Thames itself.

Our journey for the purpose of this book follows these natural features. We begin in the south-west of the county following the course of the River Wey. Its upper reaches consist of two arms that join at Tilford before flowing on past the Godalming, Guildford and Woking areas towards Weybridge. Many of the villages found here beside the river such as Elstead, Eashing, Send and Wisley are featured, and also some a little further afield but close enough to the Wey valley. We then move to the villages situated on or near the heathland in the north-west part of the county. Many of these have been affected in more recent times by the arrival of the army after it

made its base at Aldershot just over the county border in Hampshire. Included here are places such as Bagshot, Chobham, Frimley and Windlesham.

The third chapter follows the line of both the chalk and greensand hills from the west to the east. It includes not only villages and communities high up in the hills, such as Headley and Woldingham on the North Downs and Coldharbour and Friday Street in the sand hills, but also villages that lie near or at the foot of these hills; settlements that originated when ancient man found fresh water springs here. What is often referred to as the fold country, the southernmost part of Surrey, is found in the next chapter, including Chiddingfold, Alfold, Witley and Hambledon.

The course of the River Mole is traced next through the villages of Brockham and Mickleham on through Stoke D'Abernon and Cobham until the Thames is reached at Molesey. This chapter also looks at the Thames-side

SEND, *Tannery Bridge 1909* 61926

villages such as Laleham and Shepperton, and takes in Stanwell right at the northernmost tip of today's county of Surrey. The final chapter contains a selection of villages in the far south-east beyond the towns of Reigate and Redhill. We visit Nutfield, Bletchingley and Godstone, to name but three.

A book of this size cannot hope to feature every single village in Surrey. I hope that the selection is a fair one, which does indeed cover most parts of the county. Some readers may know each and every part extremely well; others may only be familiar with an area close to where they live. With today's fast motorways and railways, not to mention the close proximity to two major airports, it is now both quick and easy to leave the boundaries of Surrey in search of other places to visit. I believe, however, that there is a wealth of fascinating and beautiful places to visit in this county, not to mention an extraordinary number of wonderful villages full of charm and history and some good pubs too!

Many words have been written on the county of Surrey; my favourite writer is Eric Parker, the naturalist and broadcaster, who made his home at Hambledon in 1910. A couple of years earlier he literally walked the length and breadth of Surrey for his guidebook 'Highways and Byways in Surrey', noting all manner of interesting facts. There was not a corner of the county that he did not visit. He continued to explore the county for the rest of his life, and it is, in the main, how his Surrey looked when many of the photographs that are featured in this book were taken.

May you enjoy this selection of fine photographs of the villages of Surrey from the Francis Frith collection for many years to come.

THROUGH THE WEY VALLEY

SHOTTERMILL, *The Pond 1913* 65268

The southern arm of the River Wey passes here, yet the two ponds at Shottermill are actually in West Sussex. There were four mills hereabouts that at one time or another were involved in the making of paper, tanning hides and grinding corn. The ponds supplied extra power to one of the mill's waterwheels.

SHOTTERMILL
Critchmere 1914 67082

The view looks down Critchmere Hill with the Royal Oak pub in the distance. The area is in the far south-west corner of Surrey and is now regarded as a part of Haslemere. The writer George Bernard Shaw and his wife Charlotte spent their honeymoon at nearby Pitfold House, Woolmer Hill, in 1898.

detail of 67082

WRECCLESHAM
The Village 1907
56335

It is a sunny day in this quiet village that stands between the water meadows of the River Wey and Alice Holt Forest. Absolom Harris set up a pottery in the village in 1873, using the local deposit of blue gault clay. Today, the pottery buildings are being restored by the Farnham Trust as craft workshops, and the West Street Potters, a teaching group, continues the tradition of making ceramics.

THE BOURNE
The Village 1909 61351

The Bourne stream runs through the area of Lower, Middle and Upper Bourne, joining the River Wey at Moor Park. It was once an important hop-growing area, and today's Bat and Ball pub in Upper Bourne was where the pickers gathered to receive their hard-earned pay from the tally man.

CHURT, *The Post Office 1932* 85392

Nestling deep in a wooded valley, the tranquillity of this view is a world away from the busy A287 that runs through here today. A sign on the wall of the post office informs customers that a public telephone can be used here.

CHURT
The Pride of the Valley Hotel 1924 75320

Today the inn sign of this well-known local landmark features the former prime minister David Lloyd George, who made his home close by at Bron-y-de in 1921. In his later life he successfully farmed and grew fruit on his land, and during the Second World War sold his produce from his own shop.

FRENSHAM
The Pond 1925 77162

The Great Pond stretches over 108 acres, and in the 13th century it provided fish for the Bishop of Winchester when he dined at Farnham Castle. It was drained during the Second World War, as it would have been a navigation aid to enemy bombers.
The hotel, seen here, dates back to the 18th century, and was once called the White Horse.

FRENSHAM, *The Cross Roads 1914* 67551A

This part of Frensham is known as Millbridge. A milkman and his cart (centre right) are on the road that goes to Tilford. The heathland and the ponds in the area have long been popular with visitors and walkers alike. There is a large selection of picture postcards for sale at Mr Sturt's shop (right), no doubt featuring the fine views.

TILFORD, *The Bridge 1909* 61912

Two arms of the River Wey meet here, and an ancient bridge spans each arm. The bridges were almost certainly constructed by the monks of nearby Waverley Abbey, which was built in 1128. It was the first Cistercian abbey in England, and was dissolved in 1536. For years its stones were robbed for other buildings, but its ruins still give a glimpse of how it would have once looked.

TILFORD
The Village c1955
T49004

The Barley Mow must be one of the most perfect-looking pubs on one of the prettiest village greens anywhere. We see it here in high summer; what better place to watch a game of cricket? The scene has hardly changed, and today visitors have the added attraction of exploring the nearby Rural Life Museum.

ELSTEAD, *The Village 1906* 55621

The view looks north across this attractive village that is grouped around a small green. To the far left is Elstead Mill, once a worsted factory. An early motoring pioneer, Chaplin Court Treatt, also lived there. It has since become a pub and restaurant and for a while was named Bentleys, after the motor car.

SHACKLEFORD
The Village 1906 54167

The advertising sign on the tile-hung front of the shop is for Lascelles, Tickner & Co Ltd, a Guildford brewery that also made thirst-quenching mineral waters and ginger beer, no doubt on sale here. Sad to say, the shop has gone, and few young people today care to try the beverages that their great-grandparents loved.

detail of 54167

EASHING
The Village 1898 41806

This is another one of the ancient bridges that span these reaches of the River Wey. There are six in total: this one, two at Tilford, and one each at Elstead, Peper Harow and Unstead. In 1902, the bridge and the cottages on the right were bought by the National Trust for just £400.

SHALFORD, *The Village 1904* 51877

The 'shallow ford' owes its name to the Tillingbourne Stream that flows just beyond St Mary's Church (right), built in 1847, and then into the River Wey. A war memorial has been added since this photograph was taken. Today, traffic thunders along this road.

SHALFORD
The Village Sign 1925
77182

The village sign was erected in 1922 and depicts St Christopher, the patron saint of travellers, and a small child, traditionally, the infant Jesus, crossing a ford. The village was soon to become quite industrialised with the Vulcanised Fibre Works at nearby Broadford and also the engineering firm Nelco, in Station Road. Both are long gone, although smaller firms and businesses occupy those same sites today.

SEND, *The Post Office 1929* 81626

J & K Deadman's stores (left) would probably have sold every kind of provision you could have imagined - and more. The village grew with the industries that sprang up and prospered alongside the river and the navigation. These included Unwins print works, a tannery, the gravel pits, and three laundries.

WOKING
Old Woking Village 1898 42047

Before the railway came in 1838 and today's town began to grow, this was the centre of Woking. Here it appears as though it is completely deserted with not a soul to be seen. From the length of the shadows, perhaps it was only the photographer who was venturing out into the heat of the day.

RIPLEY
The Village 1903 49289

Ripley has an attractive wide thoroughfare, as we can see here. The pub sign is for the Ship, always, it seems, a locals' watering hole as opposed to the other inns and cafes that have catered for travellers on the London to Portsmouth road. Tedder's stores can be seen on the right, another shop selling everything - in this case groceries, china and glass, and Glen Spey whisky at 3s 6d a bottle.

OCKHAM
The Schools 1904
51588

With no village centre to speak of, except where the Gothic/Tudor-style Hautboy Inn stands, Ockham is nevertheless a pleasant community of leafy lanes. The origin of many of Ockham's mid 19th-century buildings can be traced to William, first Earl Lovelace, who lived at Ockham Park.

WISLEY
The Parish Church
c1955 W117025

The tiny church is Norman in origin, although evidence suggests that people settled here more than 4,000 years ago. The Royal Horticultural Society garden at Wisley is a popular attraction and a centre of excellence for horticulture. Eighty per cent of the homes in the village are owned by the RHS and used as accommodation for its staff.

WISLEY
The Anchor c1955
W117008

The present pub dates from 1934 and stands opposite Pyrford Lock. This is a section of the Wey Navigation that begins at Weybridge and continues to Guildford. Opened in 1653, it was the brainchild of Sir Richard Weston of Sutton Place, and was once an important transport route carrying goods from the Port of London to towns and villages in this part of Surrey.

BYFLEET, *High Road c1955* B265023

Byfleet is the last village that the River Wey passes before it joins the Thames at Weybridge. Close by is Brooklands, where there was once a famous motor-racing circuit, an airfield and aviation factories. The site now houses a business park and a retail centre, but Brooklands Museum tells the story of its historic past.

THE NORTH-WEST HEATHS

PITCH PLACE, *The Village 1908* 61138

The parish of Worplesdon takes in a number of smaller areas including Pitch Place, itself barely more than a cluster of buildings opposite a pleasant green on the A322 Bagshot Road. The white building on the end (left) is the original Ship Inn, while a motor garage has replaced the shop and cottages to the right of the inn.

WORPLESDON
The Village 1904
51901

For a few years around the turn of the 20th century, Worplesdon's cricket pitch was at the foot of Rickford Hill on the edge of the common. The cottages beside the Nonconformist chapel - now the village's United Reformed Church - have hardly altered, but there is no trace of the cricket pitch, as the site is now covered with trees and bushes.

PIRBRIGHT
The White Hart 1908
59655

For many people, the pub on the corner of the green at Pirbright will always be known by its former name. There was much local outcry when it was changed to the Moorhen a few years ago. Not to be outdone, the parish council has responded by placing a sign on the green opposite that reads 'White Hart Corner'.

BROOKWOOD
Connaught Road c1955
B232012

With a shortage of burial places in the capital, the London Necropolis Company bought 2,000 acres of heathland at Brookwood and laid out one-fifth of it as a cemetery. From 1854 onwards, the 'great and the good' and ordinary mortals too were laid to rest there. The growth of the village followed later. The Connaught Cafe, seen here on the left, is now a private house, but the post office next door remains.

BISLEY
The Church 1911
63144

Bisley's church of St John
the Baptist dates back to
the 13th century, and it
has a 15th-century porch
believed to be made
from a single oak.
Although the village now
has a number of modern
housing developments,
the church still stands in
a rural location.

WEST END
The Village Stores
c1955 W545004

There is a fine statue of General Charles Gordon of Khartoum in the grounds of Gordon School, that was built here as a boys' school in 1885. Then came houses and shops to create today's village on either side of the A322. Two of its close neighbouring communities have the unusual names of Penny Pot and Donkey Town.

BISLEY
Century Range c1955
B109021

There is another village in Bisley - that of the clubhouses and mobile homes found at the National Rifle Association's ranges. Its first meeting here took place in 1890, after it had quit its previous home on Wimbledon Common. It remains an important centre for the sport, and it has some charming Colonial-style buildings that hark back to the days of the Raj.

ASH
*The Post Office and the Village
1905* 53272

The village is largely a ribbon development along the A323 Guildford to Aldershot road and the B3411 towards Frimley. It has been influenced over the years by the coming of the Basingstoke Canal, the railway, and then, of course, by the military town of Aldershot. The site of the pond is now the forecourt of Tilthams Garage.

detail of 53272

ASH
The Greyhound 1932
84981

The Greyhound was once the only pub in Ash. By 1861 there were 16 pubs here, and it is reckoned that at least 17 other hostelries have come and gone within this parish. The fascia of the pub seen in this view has now been altered, and other changes here include the addition of a roundabout.

FRIMLEY, *The Canal 1906* 54912

The Basingstoke Canal, constructed between 1788 and 1794, was supposed to be part of a waterway linking the Thames with both the English and Bristol Channels. However, the dream fizzled out in rural Hampshire, and slowly the canal fell into disuse, although there was still some traffic on its Surrey stretches up until 1949. Here at Frimley and just visible in the distance is the aqueduct that takes it over the railway line.

FRIMLEY
The Green 1908 59650

The green remains, with several shops and a couple of pubs, ensuring that a village feel is still evident. But how many motorists notice this fact while passing through this largely built-up area that is home to a large number of commuters?

FRIMLEY
The Village 1906 55634

Today Frimley is very much absorbed into the town of Camberley, while this particular corner is a busy road junction. Frimley's most famous son is now without doubt the Rugby Union World Cup winner Jonny Wilkinson, who was born here in 1979.

BAGSHOT
The Square 1901 46848

The village was an important staging post in the heyday of horse-drawn coaches, and it is not surprising that the road across the wild heath was once the haunt of highwaymen. The signpost and gas lamp we see here (centre right) commemorates Queen Victoria's Diamond Jubilee of 1897. It was renovated and converted to electricity in 1994. Knight & Son's store looks full of tempting furnishings for the early Edwardian home.

41

BAGSHOT
High Street 1903
49257

Situated on a busy highway, Bagshot once had up to 14 inns offering accommodation for weary travellers. The one seen here on the left has an eye-catching sign to attract custom. Today, the local history society is doing sterling work recording and discovering new facts about Bagshot's rich past.

CHOBHAM
High Street c1955
C395010

The attractive heath, with its colourful heathers and gorse, reach down to a village boasting several buildings constructed of exquisite brickwork. The church of St Laurence has its own treasures too. They include an eight-sided wood-panelled font and a 13th-century chest with triple locks.

WINDLESHAM, *The Village 1909* 61451

This is how the village must have looked when the writer Eric Parker passed this way while researching his book 'Highways & Byways in Surrey', published in 1908. He liked the untamed landscape, and once met a family outside their bivouac making beehives out of straw. But he warned that the 'north-west heaths belong to the soldiers', and that here were 'all the camps, training grounds and rifle-ranges that do not belong to Aldershot'.

OTTERSHAW
The Otter Hotel c1955
O26004

The area now called Ottershaw was once a royal hunting ground within Windsor Forest. Similar to other heathland villages nearby, it grew in the 19th century as nurserymen came and improved the soil and in turn provided employment for the villagers. The original Otter pub was opened in 1803; it was replaced in 1927 by the roadhouse-style inn that stands here to this day.

ACROSS THE HILLS OF SURREY

HINDHEAD
The Punch Bowl Inn 1906 55508

That this may be a peaceful scene once again is the hope of many people campaigning for a tunnel to be built under the Devil's Punchbowl diverting the roaring A3 traffic and eliminating the bottleneck that regularly occurs at this spot. Wildlife should benefit too, and in particular that rare summer bird, the nightjar. A petrol station and flats stand on the site of the inn.

HINDHEAD
Beacon Hill 1909 61429

Beacon Hill was developed in the late 19th century for those who were in service to the wealthy folk who lived at neighbouring Hindhead. Well-known persons came to enjoy the air, that was thought to be on a par with Switzerland; they included George Bernard Shaw and Sir Arthur Conan Doyle.

RUNFOLD
The Village 1921 69947

The two cyclists appear to be freewheeling along the road through Runfold. It was once one of Farnham's hop-growing villages, and poles for the bines can be seen on the far left. Sand has been extracted from these parts for many years, and the vast pits are now being filled with waste material.

TONGHAM
*The Post Office
1921* 69940

The village stands at the foot of the Hog's Back close to Aldershot, but it is actually in the parish of Guildford. Today, Tongham is home to a thriving local business - the Hogs Back Brewery. Started in 1992 with an output of just 10 barrels of beer a week, it now produces more than 100. Its ales can be tasted in pubs across the south of England.

TONGHAM
The Village 1921
69942

Parts of Tongham still have a rural feel, especially at the crossroads. The White Hart pub (right) still stands on the corner, but this row of ramshackle shops on the left, that once included a draper's, a tobacconist and a motor-garage and cycle works, have now all gone.

SEALE, *The Village 1906* 53595

'It consists only of a few cottages, shy and red-roofed, deep among high hedges, busy dells and reedy meadows, with wheat fields and barley fields clothing the chalk slopes above.' Eric Parker's words of 100 years ago still apply today to this village lying under the Hog's Back ridge. Exploring it via the 'lower road' makes for a more interesting journey than racing along the A31 dual carriageway.

PUTTENHAM
The Village 1904 52441

If we travel east from Seale, we soon reach Puttenham. It still retains its post office and village school, and today has just over 500 inhabitants. Seen here on the right are small footbridges leading to the doorways of Rookery Cottages.

PUTTENHAM, *The Street, West End c1955* P122004

School Lane joins The Street on the left; beyond the lorry is the Good Intent pub. Puttenham is the location of Surrey's last remaining hop garden, and the village is home to a number of artists and sculptors.

COMPTON
The Post Office 1906
55102

Compton has lost its post office, which is now a private house, but it has two Christian treasures. The church of St Nicholas houses a unique double sanctuary on two levels, while the Watts Memorial Chapel is Grade I listed. The latter was founded by the artist George Frederick Watts and designed by his wife Mary. It was completed in 1904, the year in which he died.

BLACKHEATH
The Village 1906
53383

The village can be reached from a number of directions, but each one is a minor road, and consequently it remains a quiet spot. The colours of the heath are indeed dark in places, certainly when the heather is not in flower. The village war memorial is situated deep into the heath, served only by a footpath.

BLACKHEATH *1921*
70044

In 1929, the Dublin-born crime writer Freeman Wills Crofts came to live in Blackheath. His books were once as popular as those of Agatha Christie, although nowadays few people know of him or his work. Titles such as 'Murder at Guildford' and 'The 12.30 from Croydon' were penned at Blackheath. He was an accomplished musician, and played the organ at St Martin's Church (centre right).

WEST CLANDON
The Church 1904
51572

The village church is dedicated to Saint Peter and Saint Paul, and parts of it date back to the 13th century. It actually stands inside the grounds of Clandon Park. The Onslow family came here in 1642 - they once owned a good deal of land in the Guildford area. The church contains a number of memorials to the Onslows.

EAST CLANDON
The Village 1907
57867

While West Clandon with its railway station definitely has the air of a commuter village, East Clandon, facing the slope of the North Downs and surrounded by fields, still has a rural feel.
The children in the photograph would have attended the village's Church of England school, which opened in 1863. It was forced to close in 1968, as by then there were only 19 pupils.

WEST HORSLEY, *The Old Workhouse and the Pond 1904* 51581

This was indeed once the place where paupers and those down on their luck could seek food and a roof over their head. However, if they were able-bodied they had to do menial tasks to earn their keep. Four years after the 1834 Poor Law Amendment Act, the much larger Guildford Workhouse opened, doing away with this smaller poorhouse.

EFFINGHAM
The Village c1965
E26062

People first settled here at the foot of the North Downs because of the fresh water springs emerging from where the chalk meets a band of clay. Effingham expanded hundreds of years later once the railway arrived in 1885. Further growth in recent times included the addition of this row of shops in The Street, not far from the junction of the A246.

ALBURY, *The Silent Pool 1911* 63151

The upper of two pools that are fed by chalk springs has been a popular beauty spot since the 19th century. The tale about a lass who drowned here after an encounter with the wicked Prince John has been told to generations of visitors as if it were true. Alas, the Victorian writer Martin Tupper, who lived close by, penned it. The thatched arbour has recently been restored.

ALBURY
The Village c1950
A25070

Ornate chimneys dominate several of the buildings in the village. They were designed by Augustus Pugin while he was making alterations to Albury Park mansion following its acquisition in 1819 by Henry Drummond, a wealthy banker and MP. The village shop and post office, seen here, are now homes. However, another local store has recently reopened in the village after being shut for several years.

FARLEY GREEN
The Village 1927
79380

Houses lie to either side of the lane that runs through Farley Green, but it is the nearby heath where man once made his home. During the mid 19th century, the writer Martin Tupper exposed a fine Romano-British temple. Later digs by others discovered coins and pottery, and in 1995 the first proper excavation was made by English Heritage.

SHERE
The Village 1903
50268

This gem of a village is situated between the North Downs and the Greensand Ridge. Its beauty means that it has a constant stream of visitors who browse in the antique and gift shops and sit beside the clear Tillingbourne Stream. A real donkey usually heads the Palm Sunday procession to St James' Church - a lovely tradition in a village full of character.

SHERE
Middle Street 1924
75572

Middle Street leads into
Shere Lane and then on
towards the sandy hills of
The Hurtwood. The
building on the right was
once the premises of
C Baverstock, 'Shoeing &
General Smith'. Shere even
had its own fire station.
It can be seen on the right
just past the trees.

GOMSHALL
*The Post Office
and the Mill 1913*
65811

Gomshall is also on the Tillingbourne, and its single-storey water mill is uncommon in these parts. The fact that it once doubled up as the local post office is also unusual. Beautifully restored, it is now a restaurant. The mill pond has been filled in, and is now a play area for the children of families who are dining there.

GOMSHALL
The Compasses 1917
67997

The sign on the chimney breast reveals that the Compasses was once owned by the Surrey Public House Trust - a firm that owned a number of hostelries and hotels in the county. It merged with Forte Holdings Ltd in 1970 to become Trusthouses Forte. The sign shows a pair of compasses, linked to the carpentry profession. However, it is not known why this particular pub bears the name.

PEASLAKE, *The Village 1906* 53385

Peaslake has had its fair share of colourful residents down the years. These have included yeoman farmers, gipsies, smugglers, and the Victorian gentry. In the early 1900s it was the base for a number of suffragettes, who plotted all manner of activities in their bid to get women the vote.

ABINGER HAMMER
The Clock 1909 61362

The historic Grade II listed clock that overhangs the A25 was brand new when this photograph was taken. It has been damaged on a number of occasions by passing lorries. The 4ft-high figure of the blacksmith then has to be repaired by a firm that makes traditional merry-go-rounds. The footpath has now been widened and road markings added, so as to alert lorry drivers.

ABINGER HAMMER
The Village Green 1902
48545

The Tillingbourne flows past the green that today is a picturesque and popular spot, especially in summer. The building with the pitched roof was once W & G King's forge. They were also wheelwrights, undertakers and builders.

ABINGER
The Hatch Hotel 1902 48552

The inn suffered bomb damage during the Second World War, but it was the nearby church of St James that got the direct hit from a V1 flying bomb on 15 September 1944. The rector witnessed the destruction of his church while on his way to take a service. Perhaps he retired to the inn for a stiff drink!

ABINGER, *The Bottom 1924* 75245

Deep within The Hurtwood at Abinger Bottom are several stone-built cottages surrounded by pine trees. A stream, that eventually joins the Tillingbourne, runs through the hamlet. The element 'Hurt' in Hurtwood comes from the Old English word 'ceart', meaning a rough common of bracken, gorse and broom.

HOLMBURY ST MARY
Post Office Corner 1906 55590

At one time sheep from Romney Marsh in Kent were wintered here on the relatively dry sandy Surrey Hills. However, the area also attracted its fair share of sheep-stealers, smugglers and poachers, who knew the area well and could disappear into the forest at the slightest chance of being caught.

HOLMBURY ST MARY
The Post Office 1914
66766

After the railway came to the nearby town of Dorking, and also Gomshall, in the 19th century, Holmbury became a desirable place to live. Woodland was cleared to make way for a number of homes beside the few cottages that were already here. A church, shops and a village club all followed.

63

FRIDAY STREET
South End 1928 80674

Friday Street is indeed a picturesque spot, and therefore visitors are asked to park their vehicles in a car park a short walk up the road. It is also a good starting point for walkers exploring the area. The woodland is managed as much today as it was years ago, and with the National Trust owning a sizeable parcel of land here, it should be safe from any undesirable development.

WOOTON, *The Church 1919* 68828

The church of St John the Evangelist is the resting place of members of the Evelyn family, who lived at nearby Wooton House. John Evelyn (1620-1706), the noted diarist, was born and died at Wooton. He was also a founder member of The Royal Society. This view, unspoiled to this day, looks across to the North Downs and Ranmore Common.

WESTCOTT, *The Village 1925* 77133

With the growth of public motor transport after the First World War, pubs like the Prince of Wales next to a main road could cash in on regular passing trade. Judging by the sign (extreme left), it was hoped that the tea garden would bring in the customers.

COLDHARBOUR
The Village 1906
55602

The village is the highest in Surrey at 750ft above sea level; it is situated on the east side of Leith Hill. In the distance beyond the trees is the site of Anstiebury Camp, an Iron Age hill fort. Excavations have revealed that it had two ramparts. This view of the Plough Inn and the handful of cottages has hardly changed over the last 100 years.

COLDHARBOUR
The Green 1906
55599

Landslips have been known to occur here when rainfall has been exceptionally high. In December 2000, it was estimated that 400,000 cubic metres of earth was slowly moving down the side of Leith Hill. A section of road near here buckled, and it remained closed for six months. Finally, the ground was stabilised and the road was repaired. There were previous landslips at Coldharbour in 1673 and 1866.

BUCKLAND, *The School 1906* 55152

The village sits below the North Downs on the main road between Dorking and Reigate. In 1725, its then rector wrote to his bishop remarking that it had 'no chapel, no curate, no papist, no conformists, no school'. The school seen in this photograph was designed by the renowned Surrey-based architect Henry Woodyer and opened in 1862.

BUCKLAND
St Mary's Church 1900
45023

The church of St Mary has some parts that are medieval, but most of what can be seen today dates from its rebuilding between 1859 and 1860 under the supervision of Henry Woodyer. William Shearburn of Dorking carried out the building work at a cost of £2,253 - a tidy sum back then, and all raised by public subscription.

HEADLEY
The Village 1906
53540

Not far from the
beauty spot of Box
Hill is the village of
Headley, which is
surrounded by
heathland. In the
Domesday Book of
1086 the village is
recorded as 'Hallega',
meaning a clearing in
the heather. The
church of St Mary
dates from the
middle of the 19th century,
but it stands on the
site of a much older
place of worship.

WALTON ON THE HILL
Mere Pond 1932 85000A

This large village has spread
across the surrounding heath,
but there is still plenty of open
countryside hereabouts.
Under a recess on the north
wall of St Peter's Church there
is a worn effigy of a priest
named John de Walton, who
died in 1268. The Romans
frequented these parts, and
excavations have revealed a
13-room villa that was built in
the 1st century AD.

CHIPSTEAD, *St Margaret's Church 1886* 18940

When a new rector came to Chipstead's church of St Margaret in 1809, he got something of a shock. It had become quite dilapidated and very unholy indeed. Local cricketers were even using it as a pavilion, drinking beer while notching the runs into the wood of the altar. However, the rector turned things around: he did much of the restoration work himself, and stayed here for the next 50 years.

WHYTELEAFE
The Village c1960
W93041

The growth of the village can be traced back to the second half of the 19th century. Road and rail links (it has two railway stations) make it ideal commuter country. A roundabout has replaced what was once the village square.

WARLINGHAM
Ye Olde White Lyon
1903 50546

Near the green (now a public garden) are some interesting old buildings including the White Lion Inn, parts of which may date back to the 17th century. Since this photograph was taken, the age of the motor vehicle has arrived, and today this is an extremely busy road.

71

FARLEIGH, *The Common 1907*
59245

In the far north-east corner of the county, with the urban sprawl of Croydon bearing down upon it, Farleigh still holds on to its rural character with plenty of open countryside that includes a golf course. The toddler in this photograph is pulling a small perambulator made of basketwork. Other prams at this time were even made of papier-mâché.

detail of 59245

WOLDINGHAM
The Crescent c1955
W411028

A fine collection of vehicles is parked in front of the mock-Tudor-style shops that are grouped around the Crescent, off Station Road. The smallest church in Surrey is situated in Woldingham. St Agatha's measures just 30ft 3in by 20ft 2in. There has been a place of worship here for centuries, and the list of rectors goes back to 1308.

TITSEY, *Botley Hill Farmhouse c1950* T295005

Much of the land hereabouts is owned by the Titsey Foundation. This is Botley Hill Farmhouse, which has been a restaurant for a number of years. Today it is a popular pub and eatery. On 13 July 1940, Sidney Ireland of 610 Squadron became the first pilot to be killed in Surrey during the Battle of Britain. He lost control of his Spitfire and crashed in Titsey Park.

THE FOLD COUNTRY AND THE SOUTH

GRAYSWOOD, *The Village 1902* 48358

This small settlement lies to the north-east of Haslemere beside the A286. When this photograph was taken, the church was new and had not long been consecrated. A local man, Alfred Harman, paid for it, but unfortunately his wife was the first person to be buried in the churchyard. A large tombstone engraved with a ship marks the grave of the church's designer, Axel Hagg.

BROOK
The Post Office 1923
74891

Welland's, the post office and general stores, also repaired cycles, according to the sign (left). It would have been a handy place if you had suffered a puncture while on the lonely road from Witley to Haslemere. Viscount Pirrie, a director of the White Star shipping line, lived close by at Witley Park. The grounds covered a large area, and one or two gates can still be found with a star incorporated into the ironwork.

THURSLEY, *The Red Lion 1923* 74896

The countryside around here and into the Devil's Punchbowl was once the haunt of broom squires. They eked out a living cutting birch trees and heather for their besom broom handles and brushes, which were sold in country towns. They seldom left the area in which they lived, but they may well have enjoyed a pint or two in the Red Lion.

MILFORD, *Godalming Road 1906* 53567

Eric Parker was quite dismissive about Milford, describing it as 'less a village than a road', and having 'some pollarded elms and dusty jasmine'. He also believed that its future would belong to Godalming. He may be right on that point, yet some attractive buildings survive; this scene has hardly changed at all.

WITLEY
The White Hart 1906
53562

Witley has some lovely old buildings, one of them being the White Hart. It is claimed that for four days in 1305 the court of Edward I met at the inn. Church Lane, from where this photograph was taken, remains unspoiled, and its 'chocolate box' qualities ensure that it is regularly captured on camera.

WITLEY
The Village 1906
55526

The artist Helen Allingham (1848-1926) lived for seven years during the 1880s at nearby Sandhills. A number of her sought-after country cottage pictures are of buildings in the Witley area. She painted the original cottages on this site just before they were pulled down amid much outcry in 1885, and replaced by these mock-Tudor buildings.

WORMLEY
Wormley Hill 1909
61937

In the distance we can just see the imposing building of King Edward's School. It was founded in London in 1553 as Brideswell Hospital to care for destitute children. The boys' half of the school moved to Wormley in 1867, taking on its new name. The girls' school relocated here in 1952. Today it is an independent co-educational school with 480 pupils, of whom 300 are boarders.

HAMBLEDON
St Peter's Church 1904
51896

St Peter's Church was built in 1846, replacing a much earlier place of worship on this site. There are two old yew trees here, and in 2000, to mark the Millennium, numerous cuttings were taken and planted throughout the village.
The writer and naturalist Eric Parker lived nearby at Feathercombe, and is buried in the churchyard.

CHIDDINGFOLD, *The Old Thorn Tree 1933* 85504

This old hawthorn tree is mentioned as a landmark in a 500-year-old local deed. It stands in front of a row of pretty tile-hung buildings. In total, 107 buildings in the village are listed as having special historical and architectural interest.

CHIDDINGFOLD
The Village and the Pond 1902 48362

The word 'fold' means an enclosure of land for animals, and 'Chadynge's fold' may well date back to the Saxon period.
From the 14th to the 17th century, Chiddingfold was the centre of a great glass-making industry with French, Flemish and German craftsmen coming here to work.
It died out following a Royal Proclamation in 1615 prohibiting the use of wood as an industrial fuel.

BRAMLEY
High Street 1904 51892

Taken at the western end of the village, this photograph shows the Jolly Farmer pub on the right. It was formerly known as the Wheatsheaf. There is, of course, another Wheatsheaf further along the road; it had once been a pair of cottages, but they were converted to a beer house in the 1880s.

BRAMLEY
The School 1906
53607

The village school opened in 1851, but its role has changed several times over the years. In 1904 it became a mixed school of infants, juniors and seniors. From 1949, it was solely a junior school, and then switched to become a first school in 1973. Closure was threatened in 1994, yet it survives to this day with infant pupils as well as a nursery.

WONERSH
The Village 1932 84959

The half-timbered Grantley Arms pub (left) is named after Fletcher Norman, First Baron Grantley (1716-1789), a colourful character who was an MP and a rather dubious lawyer. He had married the daughter and heir to Sir William Chapple of Wonersh. The Pepperpot, on the right, is made of beams and tiles from Wonersh Park mansion. Struck by passing vehicles on a number of occasions, it now stands on a solid plinth to protect it.

SHAMLEY GREEN, *The Village 1906* 53612

The village was once known as Shamble Lea, and Oliver Cromwell granted it a charter to hold an annual fair. The well-known TV artist Tony Hart lives in Shamley Green, while Alfred Hitchcock once lived here, and Sir Richard Branson spent part of his childhood here.

SHAMLEY GREEN
The Village c1955
S103006

A community of Cokelers, a religious group otherwise known as the Dependents, once lived in the village. Founded in the 1850s, they established a number of small religious communities on the Surrey/Sussex border. Cokeler women wore black straw bonnets over their plaited buns. They had three religious services every Sunday with more in the week; they were extremely business-like, and very kind to everyone in need.

CRANLEIGH
The Village 1904
51298

There is some debate over the meaning of the name. Is it taken from the notion that the lord of the manor once bred cranes or herons for his table? Or that cranberries once grew nearby? 'Leah' is, however, a Saxon name for a clearing in a wood. Cromwell Cottage on the right gets its name as Cromwell's men were stationed there when he was in the area in 1657.

CRANLEIGH
The Shop 1906 56755

The village's name was originally spelt Cranley. The volume of mail soared after the railway came in 1865, and so as not to confuse it with Crawley, the Post Office soon had the name changed to the spelling used to this day. Collins the butcher's (left) slaughtered its own animals on the premises. The shop also sold a wide range of groceries.

EWHURST, *The Memorial 1922* 72083

Eli Hamshire (1834-1896) lived in Ewhurst all his life. Self-educated, he was a radical thinker who bombarded politicians with his thoughts on improving society. They included finding civil employment for soldiers, vaccination, brewing beer and the workhouse. The memorial contains the names of 51 Ewhurst men who died in the First World War. One wonders what Eli would have had to say about the 'war to end all wars'.

EWHURST
The Village 1925 77183

The Old Crown Inn is seen here in the days when it sold ales brewed by Lascelles, Tickner & Co, of Guildford. The pub and also the tearooms that were once next door are now private residences. The Bulls Head pub, on the opposite side of the road, remains.

ALFOLD
The Village c1950
A302001

Here we see another
Crown Inn deep in
the Fold country, and
this one is still a
licensed premises!
The road through the
village follows the
route of the Guildford
to Arundel turnpike,
completed in 1809.
Medieval glass was
also made near here
in Sidney Wood.
Jean Carre, one of the
last of the French
glassmakers to work
in these parts, is said
to be buried in Alfold
churchyard.

FOREST GREEN
The Parrot Inn 1924
75462

The area is rather
romantically referred to as
smugglers' country; it is
said to have been a kind of
halfway house between the
Sussex coast and London,
where contraband could
be safely hidden. As a folk
song goes:

'It's Champagne fine for
communion wine and the
parson drinks it too,

With a sly wink prays
'forgive these men, for they
know not what they do'.'

OAKWOOD, *The Village 1906* 53524

Well off the beaten track and close to the West Sussex border, this village is now more commonly known as Oakwoodhill. It has a delightful old church standing on its own in woodland. The Punch Bowl Inn (left) is central to the village; this is where the Surrey Union Hunt meets on Boxing Day.

OCKLEY
*The Red Lion Inn
1906* 53511

The A29 that runs in a straight line through the village follows the course of the Roman Stane Street. The name Ockley comes from 'Occa's lea' - a Saxon who made a clearing in the wood here. Four pubs are situated in Ockley, and the well and pump (foreground right) were installed in 1837 following a bequest from a wealthy governess.

OCKLEY, *The Windmill 1906* 55617

The windmill was built in 1802, and was one of a number in the south and eastern parts of the county. Known as Elmer's mill, it looks as if it was in reasonably good shape when this photograph was taken. However, it was abandoned in 1912 and finally fell down in 1944.

OCKLEY
The Post Office 1914
67032

This photograph shows the variety of services that could be found in one small place, from posting letters and buying groceries at the Surrey Trading Co's stores (centre), to Ansell's (right) operating as wheelwrights, builders and undertakers. In Ockley, there was once a community of 'illegal' weavers attempting to avoid excise regulations, an oast house for drying hops, basket makers, and even a workhouse.

CAPEL
The Crown 1924
75504

The village centre with the Crown pub and the old church is a pleasant spot. To the south of the village, brick making has been an important local industry. However, in recent years plans to build an energy-from-waste incinerator at Capel have angered residents. Although the scheme was withdrawn in 2003, it remains to be seen whether it really is the end of the saga.

BEARE GREEN
The Post Office 1924 75497

Bricks have been made here since the 19th century. In 1930, the Sussex & Dorking Brick Co, who specialised in hand-made bricks, opened a large brickworks. It was taken over by the Redland Group in 1958. Beare Green bricks form the unusual 'Brick Knot' sculpture that can be seen in the centre of Reigate.

SOUTH HOLMWOOD, *The Village 1903* 50949

The delightful green, where cricket had been played for more than 100 years, no longer exists. Today the A24 dual carriageway runs straight through it. The shop to the left was once the local butcher's.

SOUTH HOLMWOOD
The Sundial 1904
52202

The white house, known as The Sundial, had just been built when this photograph was taken. Its owners were a Mr and Mrs Pethick Lawrence, who opened it as a holiday home for poor children from London.

HOLMWOOD
*The Post Office
1906* 54886

According to Eric Parker, scores of visitors to Leith Hill would alight at Holmwood railway station and be taken by horse-drawn brake to the foot of the hill - the rest of the trip they would have to make on foot! South Holmwood's fire station was once just to the left of this picture, and the post office (extreme left), doubled up as Crofts', bakers and confectioners.

NEWDIGATE
The Six Bells 1924
75521

The pub takes its name from the number of bells at St Peter's Church that stands opposite. The church also has a long tradition of skilful bell ringers. A signboard on the open-top bus states that it is number 26, calling at Redhill, Reigate, Leigh and Parkgate.

NEWDIGATE
The Village 1906
53537

It is believed the name of the village derives from 'on-Ewood-gate' - the word 'gate' means 'road' in Middle English. The building on the right dates back to the 16th century, and was once the village shop or shops. At one time part of it was a butcher's premises, and at the time of writing, garden statuary was on sale here.

LEIGH, *The Green 1904* 52198

The small late-medieval church of St Barthomolew stands opposite a picturesque green that has not changed its appearance for many years. Yet some villagers fear the expansion plans for Gatwick Airport a few miles to the south, claiming that Leigh would become 'a noisy, polluted, traffic-clogged and over-built airport dormitory suburb.'

THE MOLE VALLEY AND THE THAMES

SALFORDS *1907* 57625

The River Mole rises in West Sussex and enters Surrey south of Gatwick Airport. One of the first villages it skirts is Salfords. The Monotype factory, which once made components for the hot metal printing trade, is still based here. It now operates in the modern computer age, and is part of the AGFA group.

BETCHWORTH
The Village 1906
55145

Travellers on the A25 cannot fail to see the scars on the south side of the North Downs that were once the Betchworth quarries. The village itself lies to the south of the main road and is therefore often overlooked. To this day it retains many quiet corners. However, the ruins of a 14th-century castle in Betchworth Park are seen even less; unfortunately there is no public access to them.

BROCKHAM
The Green c1965
B224014

Without doubt, this is one of Surrey's most picturesque villages, well known for its spectacular Bonfire Night celebrations. The 2003 event surpassed all records, with 25,000 people watching two and a half tonnes of fireworks go up in smoke, while £25,000 was raised for good causes. In this photograph the Royal Oak pub displays the well-known sign for Friary Meux.

BROCKHAM, *The Green and the Church 1900* 45017A

Christ Church, Brockham was built in 1846 and sits proudly in the centre of the village. The old water pump, seen to the right with its ornate shelter, is a reminder that mains water, something we now take for granted, is a relatively modern luxury. Water can also be a curse, and the Mole has burst its banks here in recent years.

WEST HUMBLE
The Village 1906 54693

This is perhaps the most delightfully named village in the county. Here the River Mole cuts into the steep slope of Box Hill near the Burford Bridge Hotel. Lord Nelson spent some time here in 1801, and noted in his diary what a pretty place it was.

MICKLEHAM, *The Lych Gate 1928* 80805

These vehicles are passing through the village long before today's bypass was created. On the fast A24 dual-carriageway road, signs once warned of 'deceptive bends'. The rock band 10cc, who owned a recording studio in nearby Dorking, may well have seen these signs when they named their 1977 album 'Deceptive Bends'.

FETCHAM
The River Mole 1928
80801

The River Mole has been identified as one of the UK's top watercourses, with 14 different species of fish - other rivers only have an average of eight. This is Fetcham Splash, a thoroughfare leading to a small island in the river. The wooden footbridge has been replaced by a concrete structure.

FETCHAM
The Village c1965
F168055

The parade of shops on the Cobham Road may now have different traders, but the view has not really changed over the last 40 years. The vehicles, though, place the photograph firmly in the 1960s. Once Fetcham was a village surrounded by countryside, but recent development means it is now a suburb of Leatherhead.

ASHTEAD
The Village 1913
65175

Ashtead stands beside the Rye, a tributary of the Mole, and judging by the signs for the tea gardens and a 'cyclist's rest', passing trade on the Leatherhead to Epsom road was much sought-after. The Ashtead Pottery, set up to provide employment for disabled ex-servicemen, was in business here from 1923 to 1935. It produced a range of characteristic wares that are now very collectable.

STOKE D'ABERNON
Station Road c1960
S196017

Owing to 20th century development, as seen here in Station Road, Stoke D'Abernon has merged into Cobham. However, the village does have the county's oldest church. Part of the nave and the chancel at St Mary's has walls dating back to Saxon times, and the walls incorporate many Roman bricks. It stands close to the River Mole, and now looks across the water meadows to the M25.

COBHAM
The Post Office 1911 63129

The two boys in uniform standing with their bicycles outside Cobham post office may well have been telegraph boys, ready at a moment's notice to deliver a telegram. Not far from the village was an even earlier form of communication - the semaphore tower at Chatley Heath. It was one of a series of towers built between London and Portsmouth and used in the early 19th century by the Admiralty.

detail of 63129

COBHAM
*The Village Hall,
Anyards Road 1931*
84171

Some may view Cobham today as a small town with its comprehensive range of shops and services. The hall, seen here, has now gone, and has been replaced by offices. A cobbler and engraver currently occupy the small shop on the left that was once Farrant the newsagent.

WESTON GREEN, *The Village c1955* W544009

The village is in a pleasant spot on the road from Esher to Hampton Court. Some fine old cottages and a pond border the large green and common. On the extreme right, the inn sign of the Greyhound can be seen, while another pub around the corner is currently called Shoosh.

EAST MOLESEY
The Lock 1896 38347

Here the Rivers Mole
and Ember join and
enter the Thames. Nearby
is Molesey Lock. It is
perfectly plain to see that
pleasure boating and
messing about on the river
has long been a popular
pastime. On the opposite
side of the bank is Bushy
Park, and in the distance we
can see the graceful
Hampton Court Bridge.

103

LALEHAM
The Church 1890
23596

The writer and poet Matthew Arnold (1822-88) was born in the village and is buried in the churchyard of All Saints'. He was also a great campaigner for educational reform, and was the son of Thomas Arnold, the famous headmaster of Rugby School. Once part of Middlesex, Laleham transferred to Surrey following the boundary changes of the 1970s.

SHEPPERTON, *A Backwater and the Church 1890* 23584

The Thames snakes and doubles back in these parts, and provides a delightful view of the church of St Nicholas. Navigation on the river was improved when the Desborough Channel was cut in the 1930s. The jetty leads down from Church Square, which contains some fine 18th-century buildings.

STANWELL, *St Mary's Church 1895* 36025

A little to the north of the Thames and beyond Staines is the village of Stanwell. Despite bordering Heathrow Airport with all its urbanisation, its tiny village green and some quaint cottages survive. The tower of St Mary's Church dates to the 13th century, while the shingled spire was added a hundred or so years later.

SOUTH-EASTERN SURREY

SHIPLEY BRIDGE
The Village 1929 81602

This tiny community is situated in what once must
have been one of the most remote parts of Surrey.
The M23 now cuts a swathe through the village, which
is within earshot of the aircraft taking off and landing
at nearby Gatwick Airport.

SMALLFIELD, *The Plough c1960* S664023

The village takes it name from Smallfield Place, an estate given to John de Burstow in the reign of Edward III for services rendered during the French wars. A lawyer, Edward Bysshe, enlarged the house in the 17th century, and admitted that the money came from 'fees of foolish clients'. Since this photograph was taken, the first-floor frontage of the Plough public house has been extended.

OUTWOOD
The Post Office 1906
54735

People come to Outwood to see Britain's oldest working windmill, a post mill, built in 1665. There was once a smock mill here too, but it collapsed some years ago. The Budgen family, founders of the modern grocery chain, were millers here until 1807. K Wright was the grocer in the village when this photograph was taken. The premises (left) also served as a post office, draper and outfitter, newsagent and stationer.

NUTFIELD
The Village c1955
N53012

That useful commodity fuller's earth, a non-plastic clay that has been used for centuries to clean woven woollen cloth, and more recently in the refinement of lubricating oil, was dug in and around Nutfield for hundreds of years. Some of the buildings in the village are built from a grey stone quarried from the fuller's earth pits.

NUTFIELD
The Queen's Head
1903 50705

Eric Parker described this pub as an old posting inn with the remains of what was once a spacious parlour, solid with oak beams big enough for a belfry, warmed by a broad open fireplace and offering the hospitality of two great chimney seats. The Reigate brewery of Mellersh & Neale was taken over by Meux's Brewery in 1938.

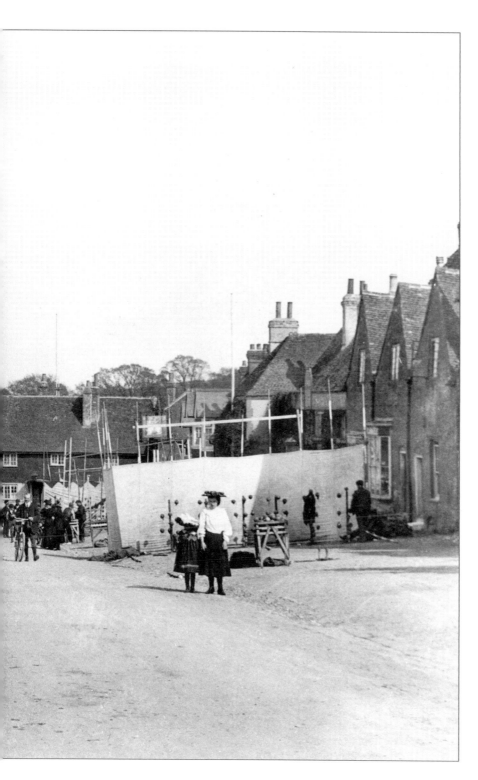

BLETCHINGLEY
Fair Day 1907 57493

Once upon a quieter time, the broad street through the village was perfect for a fair. In this view, travelling show people have arrived with their caravans and covered wagons and have set up various amusements. The village still holds its annual fair - it is now situated on Grange Meadow.

111

BLETCHINGLEY
The Village 1903
50838

In the days when the village had two MPs (before the Reform Act of 1832), election day was something to behold. Even though barely a dozen people were eligible to vote, the inns set their barrels out on the street, and it is said that 'the Bletchingley cobbles ran with beer'. The two buildings in the centre of this photograph no longer exist.

BLINDLEY HEATH, *The Village c1955* B123016

Closely hugging the A22 a few miles south of Godstone is Blindley Heath. On 28 November 1940, a German Junkers 88 crash-landed in a field near here. The aircraft was intact, but where were the crew? Years later, military records confirmed that they had bailed out when the plane developed engine trouble over northern France. It crossed the Channel on its own, and crashed when it ran out of fuel!

GODSTONE
The White Hart 1898
42751

Back in the 18th century, water that reputedly cured gout was being drawn from a well in the village that had been sunk beside a pear tree. No one could eat the fruit as it was so hard - but the Iron Peartree Water was much sought after. People came from miles around to take the cure. It could be bought at the White Hart Inn, seen here on the right, for a shilling a bottle.

GODSTONE, *Rooks Nests Lodge 1909* 61978

Rooks Nest was the home of Sir George Gilbert Scott (1811-78), leader of the Gothic revival in architecture, a style that befitted small country churches as well as major metropolitan landmarks. He carried out hundreds of church restorations as well as designing public buildings, including St Pancras Station Hotel in London. His grandson, Sir Giles Gilbert Scott, designed the K6 - Britain's famous red telephone box.

TANDRIDGE
The Post Office 1906
55416

Tandridge is a quiet village spread along a minor road to the east of Godstone. This post office was, no doubt, well stocked in the days when the photograph was taken. Visitors sending a greetings card home may well have mentioned the massive yew tree in the churchyard, believed to be about 1,000 years old.

OXTED
High Street 1908
59625

The BBC used to come to the countryside around Oxted to record and broadcast the sound of nightingales. Although there has been much expansion in Oxted, this part, known as Old Oxted, has retained much of its charm. There are a number of inns still open, including the Crown, seen here on the right.

LIMPSFIELD
The Village 1906
54258

A number of interesting half-timbered and tile-hung cottages can be found in this village, which lies just to the south of the M25. Music lovers come to visit the grave of the composer Frederick Delius, who is buried in St Peter's churchyard. He died in France in 1934, but a year later his body was brought back to England and laid to rest here following a torchlight funeral oration.

LINGFIELD
The Old Cage and the Pond 1904 52989

The landmark building that stands in the centre of the village was for many years the lock-up. It was built in 1773, and was last used in 1882. Perhaps the gentleman leaning on his stick (left) would have recalled when people either the worse for drink or perhaps even accused of poaching were held there before facing the local magistrate.

DORMANSLAND, *The Schools 1910* 62812

The county runs out here: the roads from Dormansland lead a short way to the border with either Kent or Sussex. The name seems apt if there ever was a 'doorman' here guarding the entrance into Surrey! The village school is now on a new site, and the old buildings have been demolished and replaced by houses.

INDEX

Frith Book Co Titles

www.francisfrith.co.uk

The Frith Book Company publishes over 100 new titles each year. A selection of those currently available is listed below. For latest catalogue please contact Frith Book Co.
Town Books 96 pages, approximately 100 photos. **County and Themed Books** 128 pages, approximately 150 photos (unless specified). All titles hardback with laminated case and jacket, except those indicated pb (paperback)

Title	ISBN	Price	Title	ISBN	Price
Amersham, Chesham & Rickmansworth (pb)	1-85937-340-2	£9.99	Devon (pb)	1-85937-297-x	£9.99
Andover (pb)	1-85937-292-9	£9.99	Devon Churches (pb)	1-85937-250-3	£9.99
Aylesbury (pb)	1-85937-227-9	£9.99	Dorchester (pb)	1-85937-307-0	£9.99
Barnstaple (pb)	1-85937-300-3	£9.99	Dorset (pb)	1-85937-269-4	£9.99
Basildon Living Memories (pb)	1-85937-515-4	£9.99	Dorset Coast (pb)	1-85937-299-6	£9.99
Bath (pb)	1-85937-419-0	£9.99	Dorset Living Memories (pb)	1-85937-584-7	£9.99
Bedford (pb)	1-85937-205-8	£9.99	Down the Severn (pb)	1-85937-560-x	£9.99
Bedfordshire Living Memories	1-85937-513-8	£14.99	Down The Thames (pb)	1-85937-278-3	£9.99
Belfast (pb)	1-85937-303-8	£9.99	Down the Trent	1-85937-311-9	£14.99
Berkshire (pb)	1-85937-191-4	£9.99	East Anglia (pb)	1-85937-265-1	£9.99
Berkshire Churches	1-85937-170-1	£17.99	East Grinstead (pb)	1-85937-138-8	£9.99
Berkshire Living Memories	1-85937-332-1	£14.99	East London	1-85937-080-2	£14.99
Black Country	1-85937-497-2	£12.99	East Sussex (pb)	1-85937-606-1	£9.99
Blackpool (pb)	1-85937-393-3	£9.99	Eastbourne (pb)	1-85937-399-2	£9.99
Bognor Regis (pb)	1-85937-431-x	£9.99	Edinburgh (pb)	1-85937-193-0	£8.99
Bournemouth (pb)	1-85937-545-6	£9.99	England In The 1880s	1-85937-331-3	£17.99
Bradford (pb)	1-85937-204-x	£9.99	Essex - Second Selection	1-85937-456-5	£14.99
Bridgend (pb)	1-85937-386-0	£7.99	Essex (pb)	1-85937-270-8	£9.99
Bridgwater (pb)	1-85937-305-4	£9.99	Essex Coast	1-85937-342-9	£14.99
Bridport (pb)	1-85937-327-5	£9.99	Essex Living Memories	1-85937-490-5	£14.99
Brighton (pb)	1-85937-192-2	£8.99	Exeter	1-85937-539-1	£9.99
Bristol (pb)	1-85937-264-3	£9.99	Exmoor (pb)	1-85937-608-8	£9.99
British Life A Century Ago (pb)	1-85937-213-9	£9.99	Falmouth (pb)	1-85937-594-4	£9.99
Buckinghamshire (pb)	1-85937-200-7	£9.99	Folkestone (pb)	1-85937-124-8	£9.99
Camberley (pb)	1-85937-222-8	£9.99	Frome (pb)	1-85937-317-8	£9.99
Cambridge (pb)	1-85937-422-0	£9.99	Glamorgan	1-85937-488-3	£14.99
Cambridgeshire (pb)	1-85937-420-4	£9.99	Glasgow (pb)	1-85937-190-6	£9.99
Cambridgeshire Villages	1-85937-523-5	£14.99	Glastonbury (pb)	1-85937-338-0	£7.99
Canals And Waterways (pb)	1-85937-291-0	£9.99	Gloucester (pb)	1-85937-232-5	£9.99
Canterbury Cathedral (pb)	1-85937-179-5	£9.99	Gloucestershire (pb)	1-85937-561-8	£9.99
Cardiff (pb)	1-85937-093-4	£9.99	Great Yarmouth (pb)	1-85937-426-3	£9.99
Carmarthenshire (pb)	1-85937-604-5	£9.99	Greater Manchester (pb)	1-85937-266-x	£9.99
Chelmsford (pb)	1-85937-310-0	£9.99	Guildford (pb)	1-85937-410-7	£9.99
Cheltenham (pb)	1-85937-095-0	£9.99	Hampshire (pb)	1-85937-279-1	£9.99
Cheshire (pb)	1-85937-271-6	£9.99	Harrogate (pb)	1-85937-423-9	£9.99
Chester (pb)	1-85937-382 8	£9.99	Hastings and Bexhill (pb)	1-85937-131-0	£9.99
Chesterfield (pb)	1-85937-378-x	£9.99	Heart of Lancashire (pb)	1-85937-197-3	£9.99
Chichester (pb)	1-85937-228-7	£9.99	Helston (pb)	1-85937-214-7	£9.99
Churches of East Cornwall (pb)	1-85937-249-x	£9.99	Hereford (pb)	1-85937-175-2	£9.99
Churches of Hampshire (pb)	1-85937-207-4	£9.99	Herefordshire (pb)	1-85937-567-7	£9.99
Cinque Ports & Two Ancient Towns	1-85937-492-1	£14.99	Herefordshire Living Memories	1-85937-514-6	£14.99
Colchester (pb)	1-85937-188-4	£8.99	Hertfordshire (pb)	1-85937-247-3	£9.99
Cornwall (pb)	1-85937-229-5	£9.99	Horsham (pb)	1-85937-432-8	£9.99
Cornwall Living Memories	1-85937-248-1	£14.99	Humberside (pb)	1-85937-605-3	£9.99
Cotswolds (pb)	1-85937-230-9	£9.99	Hythe, Romney Marsh, Ashford (pb)	1-85937-256-2	£9.99
Cotswolds Living Memories	1-85937-255-4	£14.99	Ipswich (pb)	1-85937-424-7	£9.99
County Durham (pb)	1-85937-398-4	£9.99	Isle of Man (pb)	1-85937-268-6	£9.99
Croydon Living Memories (pb)	1-85937-162-0	£9.99	Isle of Wight (pb)	1-85937-429-8	£9.99
Cumbria (pb)	1-85937-621-5	£9.99	Isle of Wight Living Memories	1-85937-304-6	£14.99
Derby (pb)	1-85937-367-4	£9.99	Kent (pb)	1-85937-189-2	£9.99
Derbyshire (pb)	1-85937-196-5	£9.99	Kent Living Memories(pb)	1-85937-401-8	£9.99
Derbyshire Living Memories	1-85937-330-5	£14.99	Kings Lynn (pb)	1-85937-334-8	£9.99

Available from your local bookshop or from the publisher

Frith Book Co Titles (continued)

Lake District (pb)	1-85937-275-9	£9.99	Sherborne (pb)	1-85937-301-1	£9.99
Lancashire Living Memories	1-85937-335-6	£14.99	Shrewsbury (pb)	1-85937-325-9	£9.99
Lancaster, Morecambe, Heysham (pb)	1-85937-233-3	£9.99	Shropshire (pb)	1-85937-326-7	£9.99
Leeds (pb)	1-85937-202-3	£9.99	Shropshire Living Memories	1-85937-643-6	£14.99
Leicester (pb)	1-85937-381-x	£9.99	Somerset	1-85937-153-1	£14.99
Leicestershire & Rutland Living Memories	1-85937-500-6	£12.99	South Devon Coast	1-85937-107-8	£14.99
Leicestershire (pb)	1-85937-185-x	£9.99	South Devon Living Memories (pb)	1-85937-609-6	£9.99
Lighthouses	1-85937-257-0	£9.99	South East London (pb)	1-85937-263-5	£9.99
Lincoln (pb)	1-85937-380-1	£9.99	South Somerset	1-85937-318-6	£14.99
Lincolnshire (pb)	1-85937-433-6	£9.99	South Wales	1-85937-519-7	£14.99
Liverpool and Merseyside (pb)	1-85937-234-1	£9.99	Southampton (pb)	1-85937-427-1	£9.99
London (pb)	1-85937-183-3	£9.99	Southend (pb)	1-85937-313-5	£9.99
London Living Memories	1-85937-454-9	£14.99	Southport (pb)	1-85937-425-5	£9.99
Ludlow (pb)	1-85937-176-0	£9.99	St Albans (pb)	1-85937-341-0	£9.99
Luton (pb)	1-85937-235-x	£9.99	St Ives (pb)	1-85937-415-8	£9.99
Maidenhead (pb)	1-85937-339-9	£9.99	Stafford Living Memories (pb)	1-85937-503-0	£9.99
Maidstone (pb)	1-85937-391-7	£9.99	Staffordshire (pb)	1-85937-308-9	£9.99
Manchester (pb)	1-85937-198-1	£9.99	Stourbridge (pb)	1-85937-530-8	£9.99
Marlborough (pb)	1-85937-336-4	£9.99	Stratford upon Avon (pb)	1-85937-388-7	£9.99
Middlesex	1-85937-158-2	£14.99	Suffolk (pb)	1-85937-221-x	£9.99
Monmouthshire	1-85937-532-4	£14.99	Suffolk Coast (pb)	1-85937-610-x	£9.99
New Forest (pb)	1-85937-390-9	£9.99	Surrey (pb)	1-85937-240-6	£9.99
Newark (pb)	1-85937-366-6	£9.99	Surrey Living Memories	1-85937-328-3	£14.99
Newport, Wales (pb)	1-85937-258-9	£9.99	Sussex (pb)	1-85937-184-1	£9.99
Newquay (pb)	1-85937-421-2	£9.99	Sutton (pb)	1-85937-337-2	£9.99
Norfolk (pb)	1-85937-195-7	£9.99	Swansea (pb)	1-85937-167-1	£9.99
Norfolk Broads	1-85937-486-7	£14.99	Taunton (pb)	1-85937-314-3	£9.99
Norfolk Living Memories (pb)	1-85937-402-6	£9.99	Tees Valley & Cleveland (pb)	1-85937-623-1	£9.99
North Buckinghamshire	1-85937-626-6	£14.99	Teignmouth (pb)	1-85937-370-4	£7.99
North Devon Living Memories	1-85937-261-9	£14.99	Thanet (pb)	1-85937-116-7	£9.99
North Hertfordshire	1-85937-547-2	£14.99	Tiverton (pb)	1-85937-178-7	£9.99
North London (pb)	1-85937-403-4	£9.99	Torbay (pb)	1-85937-597-9	£9.99
North Somerset	1-85937-302-x	£14.99	Truro (pb)	1-85937-598-7	£9.99
North Wales (pb)	1-85937-298-8	£9.99	Victorian & Edwardian Dorset	1-85937-254-6	£14.99
North Yorkshire (pb)	1-85937-236-8	£9.99	Victorian & Edwardian Kent (pb)	1-85937-624-X	£9.99
Northamptonshire Living Memories	1-85937-529-4	£14.99	Victorian & Edwardian Maritime Album (pb)	1-85937-622-3	£9.99
Northamptonshire	1-85937-150-7	£14.99	Victorian and Edwardian Sussex (pb)	1-85937-625-8	£9.99
Northumberland Tyne & Wear (pb)	1-85937-281-3	£9.99	Villages of Devon (pb)	1-85937-293-7	£9.99
Northumberland	1-85937-522-7	£14.99	Villages of Kent (pb)	1-85937-294-5	£9.99
Norwich (pb)	1-85937-194-9	£8.99	Villages of Sussex (pb)	1-85937-295-3	£9.99
Nottingham (pb)	1-85937-324-0	£9.99	Warrington (pb)	1-85937-507-3	£9.99
Nottinghamshire (pb)	1-85937-187-6	£9.99	Warwick (pb)	1-85937-518-9	£9.99
Oxford (pb)	1-85937-411-5	£9.99	Warwickshire (pb)	1-85937-203-1	£9.99
Oxfordshire (pb)	1-85937-430-1	£9.99	Welsh Castles (pb)	1-85937-322-4	£9.99
Oxfordshire Living Memories	1-85937-525-1	£14.99	West Midlands (pb)	1-85937-289-9	£9.99
Paignton (pb)	1-85937-374-7	£7.99	West Sussex (pb)	1-85937-607-x	£9.99
Peak District (pb)	1-85937-280-5	£9.99	West Yorkshire (pb)	1-85937-201-5	£9.99
Pembrokeshire	1-85937-262-7	£14.99	Weston Super Mare (pb)	1-85937-306-2	£9.99
Penzance (pb)	1-85937-595-2	£9.99	Weymouth (pb)	1-85937-209-0	£9.99
Peterborough (pb)	1-85937-219-8	£9.99	Wiltshire (pb)	1-85937-277-5	£9.99
Picturesque Harbours	1-85937-208-2	£14.99	Wiltshire Churches (pb)	1-85937-171-x	£9.99
Piers	1-85937-237-6	£17.99	Wiltshire Living Memories (pb)	1-85937-396-8	£9.99
Plymouth (pb)	1-85937-389-5	£9.99	Winchester (pb)	1-85937-428-x	£9.99
Poole & Sandbanks (pb)	1-85937-251-1	£9.99	Windsor (pb)	1-85937-333-x	£9.99
Preston (pb)	1-85937-212-0	£9.99	Wokingham & Bracknell (pb)	1-85937-329-1	£9.99
Reading (pb)	1-85937-238-4	£9.99	Woodbridge (pb)	1-85937-498-0	£9.99
Redhill to Reigate (pb)	1-85937-596-0	£9.99	Worcester (pb)	1-85937-165-5	£9.99
Ringwood (pb)	1-85937-384-4	£7.99	Worcestershire Living Memories	1-85937-489-1	£14.99
Romford (pb)	1-85937-319-4	£9.99	Worcestershire	1-85937-152-3	£14.99
Royal Tunbridge Wells (pb)	1-85937-504-9	£9.99	York (pb)	1-85937-199-x	£9.99
Salisbury (pb)	1-85937-239-2	£9.99	Yorkshire (pb)	1-85937-186-8	£9.99
Scarborough (pb)	1-85937-379-8	£9.99	Yorkshire Coastal Memories	1-85937-506-5	£14.99
Sevenoaks and Tonbridge (pb)	1-85937-392-5	£9.99	Yorkshire Dales	1-85937-502-2	£14.99
Sheffield & South Yorks (pb)	1-85937-267-8	£9.99	Yorkshire Living Memories (pb)	1-85937-397-6	£9.99

See Frith books on the internet at www.francisfrith.co.uk

FRITH PRODUCTS & SERVICES

Francis Frith would doubtless be pleased to know that the pioneering publishing venture he started in 1860 still continues today. Over a hundred and forty years later, The Francis Frith Collection continues in the same innovative tradition and is now one of the foremost publishers of vintage photographs in the world. Some of the current activities include:

Interior Decoration

Today Frith's photographs can be seen framed and as giant wall murals in thousands of pubs, restaurants, hotels, banks, retail stores and other public buildings throughout the country. In every case they enhance the unique local atmosphere of the places they depict and provide reminders of gentler days in an increasingly busy and frenetic world.

Product Promotions

Frith products are used by many major companies to promote the sales of their own products or to reinforce their own history and heritage. Frith promotions have been used by Hovis bread, Courage beers, Scots Porage Oats, Colman's mustard, Cadbury's foods, Mellow Birds coffee, Dunhill pipe tobacco, Guinness, and Bulmer's Cider.

Genealogy and Family History

As the interest in family history and roots grows world-wide, more and more people are turning to Frith's photographs of Great Britain for images of the towns, villages and streets where their ancestors lived; and, of course, photographs of the churches and chapels where their ancestors were christened, married and buried are an essential part of every genealogy tree and family album.

Frith Products

All Frith photographs are available Framed or just as Mounted Prints and Posters (size 23 x 16 inches). These may be ordered from the address below. From time to time other products - Address Books, Calendars, Table Mats, etc - are available.

The Internet

Already fifty thousand Frith photographs can be viewed and purchased on the internet through the Frith websites and a myriad of partner sites.

For more detailed information on Frith companies and products, look at these sites:

www.francisfrith.co.uk
www.francisfrith.com
(for North American visitors)

See the complete list of Frith Books at:

www.francisfrith.co.uk

This web site is regularly updated with the latest list of publications from the Frith Book Company. If you wish to buy books relating to another part of the country that your local bookshop does not stock, you may purchase on-line.

For further information, trade, or author enquiries please contact us at the address below:
The Francis Frith Collection, Frith's Barn, Teffont, Salisbury, Wiltshire, England SP3 5QP.
Tel: +44 (0)1722 716 376 Fax: +44 (0)1722 716 881 Email: sales@francisfrith.co.uk

See Frith books on the internet at www.francisfrith.co.uk

FREE PRINT OF YOUR CHOICE

Mounted Print
Overall size 14 x 11 inches (355 x 280mm)

Choose any Frith photograph in this book.
Simply complete the Voucher opposite and return it with your remittance for £2.25 (to cover postage and handling) and we will print the photograph of your choice in SEPIA (size 11 x 8 inches) and supply it in a cream mount with a burgundy rule line (overall size 14 x 11 inches).
Please note: photographs with a reference number starting with a "Z" are not Frith photographs and cannot be supplied under this offer.
Offer valid for delivery to UK addresses only.

PLUS: **Order additional Mounted Prints at HALF PRICE - £7.49 each** (normally £14.99)
If you would like to order more Frith prints from this book, possibly as gifts for friends and family, you can buy them at half price (with no additional postage and handling costs).

PLUS: **Have your Mounted Prints framed**
For an extra £14.95 per print you can have your mounted print(s) framed in an elegant polished wood and gilt moulding, overall size 16 x 13 inches (no additional postage and handling required).

IMPORTANT!

These special prices are only available if you use this form to order . You must use the ORIGINAL VOUCHER on this page (no copies permitted). We can only despatch to one address. This offer cannot be combined with any other offer.

Send completed Voucher form to:
The Francis Frith Collection, Frith's Barn, Teffont, Salisbury, Wiltshire SP3 5QP

CHOOSE A PHOTOGRAPH FROM THIS BOOK

Voucher for **FREE** and Reduced Price Frith Prints

Please do not photocopy this voucher. Only the original is valid, so please fill it in, cut it out and return it to us with your order.

Picture ref no	Page no	Qty	Mounted @ £7.49	Framed + £14.95	Total Cost
		1	Free of charge*	£	£
			£7.49	£	£
			£7.49	£	£
			£7.49	£	£
			£7.49	£	£
			£7.49	£	£

Please allow 28 days for delivery

* Post & handling (UK)	£2.25
Total Order Cost	£

Title of this book . . . .

I enclose a cheque/postal order for £ . . . .
made payable to 'The Francis Frith Collection'

OR please debit my Mastercard / Visa / Switch (Maestro) /Amex card
(credit cards please on all overseas orders), details below

Card Number

Issue No (Switch only)   Valid from (Amex/Switch)

Expires   Signature

Name Mr/Mrs/Ms . . . .
Address . . . .
. . . .
. . . .
. . . . Postcode . . . .
Daytime Tel No . . . .
Email . . . .

Valid to 31/12/07

Would you like to find out more about Francis Frith?

We have recently recruited some entertaining speakers who are happy to visit local groups, clubs and societies to give an illustrated talk documenting Frith's travels and photographs. If you are a member of such a group and are interested in hosting a presentation, we would love to hear from you.

Our speakers bring with them a small selection of our local town and county books, together with sample prints. They are happy to take orders. A small proportion of the order value is donated to the group who have hosted the presentation. The talks are therefore an excellent way of fundraising for small groups and societies.

Can you help us with information about any of the Frith photographs in this book?

We are gradually compiling an historical record for each of the photographs in the Frith archive. It is always fascinating to find out the names of the people shown in the pictures, as well as insights into the shops, buildings and other features depicted.

If you recognize anyone in the photographs in this book, or if you have information not already included in the author's caption, do let us know. We would love to hear from you, and will try to publish it in future books or articles.

Our production team

Frith books are produced by a small dedicated team at offices in the converted Grade II listed 18th-century barn at Teffont near Salisbury, illustrated above. Most have worked with the Frith Collection for many years. All have in common one quality: they have a passion for the Frith Collection. The team is constantly expanding, but currently includes:

Paul Baron, Jason Buck, John Buck, Ruth Butler, Heather Crisp, David Davies, Isobel Hall, Julian Hight, Peter Horne, James Kinnear, Karen Kinnear, Tina Leary, Stuart Login, David Marsh, Sue Molloy, Glenda Morgan, Wayne Morgan, Kate Rotondetto, Dean Scource, Eliza Sackett, Terence Sackett, Sandra Sampson, Adrian Sanders, Sandra Sanger, Julia Skinner, Lewis Taylor, Shelley Tolcher, Lorraine Tuck and Jeremy Walker.

Free Print – see overleaf